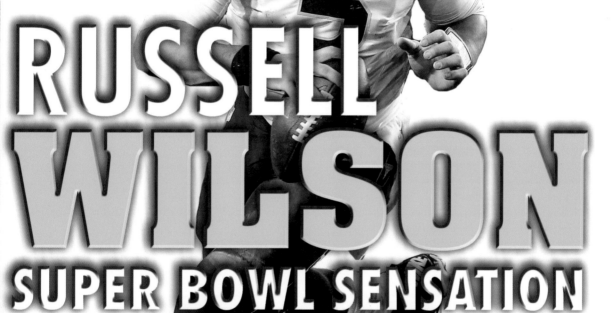

RUSSELL
WILSON
SUPER BOWL SENSATION

PETE SCHAUER

Britannica
Educational Publishing

IN ASSOCIATION WITH

ROSEN
EDUCATIONAL SERVICES

Published in 2016 by Britannica Educational Publishing (a trademark of Encyclopædia Britannica, Inc.) in association with The Rosen Publishing Group, Inc.

29 East 21st Street, New York, NY 10010

Distributed exclusively by Rosen Publishing.

To see additional Britannica Educational Publishing titles, go to rosenpublishing.com.

First Edition

Britannica Educational Publishing

J. E. Luebering: Director, Core Reference Group

Anthony L. Green: Editor, Compton's by Britannica

Rosen Publishing

Hope Lourie Killcoyne: Executive Editor

Shalini Saxena: Editor

Nelson Sá: Art Director

Designer: Nicole Russo

Cindy Reiman: Photography Manager

Library of Congress Cataloging-in-Publication Data

Schauer, Peter J.

Russell Wilson: Super Bowl sensation/Pete Schauer.—First Edition.

    pages cm.—(Living Legends of Sports)

Includes bibliographical references and index.

ISBN 978-1-68048-114-3 (Library bound)—ISBN 978-1-68048-115-0 (Paperback)—ISBN 978-1-68048-117-4 (6-pack)

1. Wilson, Russell, 1988– –Juvenile literature. 2. Football players—United States—Biography--Juvenile literature. 3. Quarterbacks (Football)—United States—Biography—Juvenile literature. I. Title.

GV939.W545S33 2015

796.332092—dc23

[B]

2014039771

Manufactured in the United States of America

CONTENTS

20 -30 -40 50 40 - 30 - 20

INTRO-DUCTION

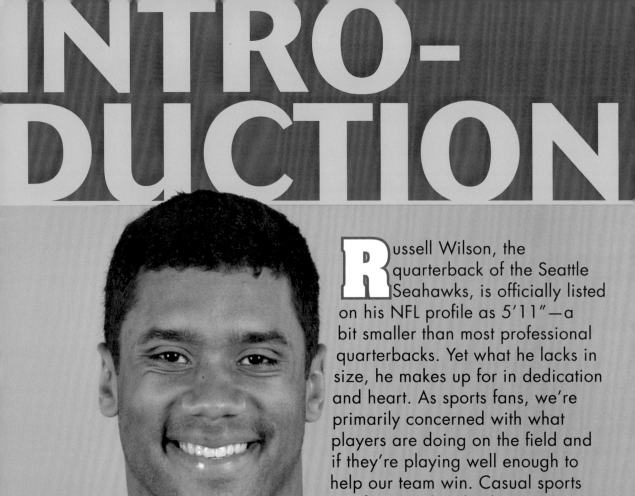

Russell Wilson, the quarterback of the Seattle Seahawks, is officially listed on his NFL profile as 5'11"—a bit smaller than most professional quarterbacks. Yet what he lacks in size, he makes up for in dedication and heart. As sports fans, we're primarily concerned with what players are doing on the field and if they're playing well enough to help our team win. Casual sports fans rarely take the time to get to know athletes and see

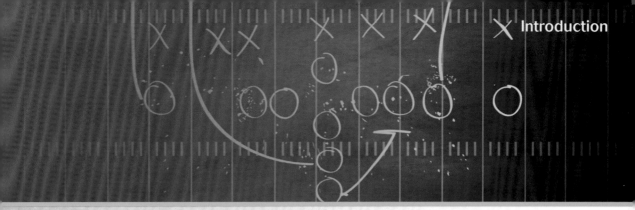

that there's more to these men and women than their performance on the field or court. But Wilson is a man that everyone can root for in all aspects of life—especially off the field.

Wilson rose to fame when he led the Seahawks to their first Super Bowl title in 2014 as a second-year quarterback. In 2015 the Seahawks returned to the Super Bowl, thanks in large part to Wilson's remarkable play in the NFC Championship game. Although the Seahawks fell short of a second title, Wilson again proved himself to be an essential part of the team.

Wilson's life outside the stadium has earned him a great deal of admiration, too. In addition to outreach work at hospitals and teen shelters, Wilson has stood up for many causes, including domestic violence and diabetes awareness. Wilson is more than just a two-time Pro Bowler and Super Bowl–winning quarterback—he's a role model for both children and adults because of his hard work, dedication, generosity, and charity, in addition to his athletic ability. His talent as a dual-threat quarterback and his generosity as a humanitarian have quickly made him a standout athlete—and a living legend of the NFL.

Despite his small stature, Wilson has continuously impressed NFL analysts and fans with his work both on and off the field.

Bringing Up a Legend

Russell Wilson was born in Cincinnati, Ohio, on November 29, 1988. But his story begins in Richmond, Virginia, where he grew up in a tight-knit family that was both athletic and educated. All it takes is one look at Wilson's family and it's easy to see where he got his athletic ability and his intelligence. His grandfather, Harrison B. Wilson, Jr., was a star athlete at Kentucky State University and later became the president of Norfolk State University. Wilson's father, Harrison B. Wilson III, attended Dartmouth College and later met his wife, Tammy, at the University of Virginia School of Law. While at Dartmouth, Harrison III played football and baseball, and he later made the San Diego Chargers' preseason team as a wide receiver. Athleticism—especially in football—lives within the Wilson family. At the age of four, a young Russell Wilson began playing football with his older brother, Harrison IV.

Like the rest of his family, Wilson realized the importance of education and made time for both his studies and athletics.

A Family Affair

From a young age, Wilson was bred to play the game of football. Russell and his brother would play with their father on the grass at the Collegiate School—a school where Russell would eventually become an All-State player. Harrison IV credits those Collegiate School days with their father for helping Russell develop his throwing skills. Harrison IV was quite an athlete himself, playing both football and baseball at the University of Richmond.

QUICK FACT

Wilson's grandfather, Harrison B. Wilson, Jr., competed in football, basketball, baseball, and track at Kentucky State University. He made a living as a professor and basketball coach before serving as president of Norfolk State University for more than 20 years.

Wilson and his brother, Harrison IV, credit their father with helping them develop their throwing skills.

In addition to playing football with his son, Wilson's father would test young Russell on different aspects of the game and why he made decisions in certain situations—something that has helped to shape Wilson into the smart and attentive player that he is today. As part of the preparation, Wilson's dad would pretend to be a TV reporter and ask his son questions, which is reflected today in Wilson's ability to handle the media during press conferences. Wilson's father embodied what a role model should be, and those qualities were instilled in Russell.

Wilson carries himself extremely well during press conferences thanks to his father, who used to act as a television reporter and quiz his son.

Russell became a devout Christian at the age of 14 after he had a dream in which his father died and Jesus told him, "You need to find out more about me." Unfortunately for Wilson, part of his dream became reality a few years later when his father died of diabetes in 2010. After Wilson lost his father, he would write "Dad" on the tape on his wrists before every college football game in which he played, to remind himself whom he was playing for.

QUICK FACT

Wilson's father, Harrison B. Wilson III, had a short stint in the NFL, playing as a wide receiver for the San Diego Chargers during the 1980 preseason.

After losing his father to diabetes in 2010, Wilson honored him by writing "Dad" on the tape on his wrists before every college game.

Confronting Challenges

Despite being brought up in an academic household, Wilson still struggled with his studies. According to his mother, when Wilson was in middle school, he traded his athletic ability for academic help from his peers. Wilson would practice any sport with friends and classmates who wanted to play or improve their game in return for their help with studying and understanding his homework. The fact that Wilson realized that he needed help with school, and that he knew how important his education was, is a direct reflection of his upbringing. He knew he may not always be able to make a living out of professional sports, so focusing on his studies was the right move.

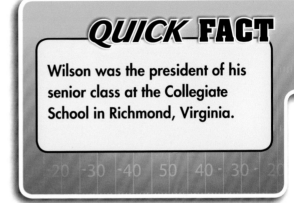

QUICK-FACT

Wilson was the president of his senior class at the Collegiate School in Richmond, Virginia.

Turning Hard Work into Success

L egends certainly aren't made overnight, and it took a lot of hard work, dedication, and persistence for Russell Wilson to make it to where he is today. Most quarterbacks—whether amateur or professional—aren't known for their running abilities. They play the quarterback position because they have strong and accurate arms. Wilson, though, worked to perfect both his passing and his running skills in high school and college, making him a double threat. This gave Wilson an advantage over other quarterbacks and really helped him excel.

Early Achievements

Wilson's career began to blossom at the Collegiate School, a K–12 prep school, where he was a standout quarterback. His reputation really began to grow in 2005 when, as a junior, he threw for 3,287 yards and 40 touchdowns while also rushing for 634 yards and 15 touchdowns, leading his team to a perfect 11–0 record. For his exceptional performance, Wilson was named an All-District, All-Region, and All-State

Highly skilled as both a passer and a runner, Wilson is one of the most dangerous double-threat quarterbacks in the NFL today.

player. This was just the beginning of the accolades that Wilson would accumulate during his career.

The following season as a senior, Wilson tossed for 3,009 yards and rushed for another 1,132. He completed nearly 60 percent of his

Wilson is shown here in 2006, when he was named the *Richmond Times-Dispatch* Player of the Year for the second time.

passes and threw for 34 touchdowns and only seven interceptions while scoring 18 rushing touchdowns. Wilson's ability to beat the defense resulted in him being named All-State, All-Conference, and Conference Player of the Year. The 2006 season concluded with the state title game in which Wilson put on one of the best performances of his career—at any level. Not only did he throw for 291 yards and two touchdowns, but he rushed for an amazing 223 yards and three more touchdowns while leading his team to a 38–17 victory—receiving his second state title in as many years. For his incredible play in the title game, Wilson appeared in *Sports Illustrated*'s "Faces in the Crowd" section, which features exceptional amateur athletes from around the nation.

QUICK FACT

Twice during his high school years, Wilson was named the *Richmond Times-Dispatch* Player of the Year.

When he wasn't playing football, Wilson kept busy with basketball and baseball. As a shortstop on Collegiate's baseball team, he batted a stellar .467 in his senior year.

Leading the Wolfpack

When it was time for college, Wilson opted for North Carolina State University in Raleigh, North Carolina. He spent his first four years of college at NC State, and despite often being told that he wasn't tall enough to play the quarterback position, Wilson overcame the odds against him. After being named to the Atlantic Coast Conference (ACC) Academic Honor Roll and redshirting (delaying his playing time in order to lengthen his eligibility) during his freshman year in 2007, Wilson took his first snap in his second year of college. He split time at quarterback for the first five games of the season before beating out senior Daniel Evans and junior Harrison Beck for the starting job. For his excellent 2008 season—which was highlighted by 1,955 yards passing, 17 touchdowns, and just one interception—Wilson was named first-team All-ACC quarterback. It

The football program at NC State has produced many NFL players, including J.R. Sweezy, Wilson's Seahawks teammate, and Mario Williams, a defensive end for the Buffalo Bills.

was the first time that a freshman player had been handed that award by the ACC. Wilson was also named the ACC Rookie of the Year.

Wilson's 2009 campaign was just as impressive as his previous year. He led the ACC with 31 touchdown passes, racked up 3,287 yards of total offense (passing and rushing combined), and set the NCAA record for most pass attempts without an interception (379). He was also named to the All-ACC Academic Football Team.

As Wilson's athletic career really began to blossom, his studies and education never wavered. Wilson graduated from NC State in three years with a bachelor's degree in communications and continued his education during the 2010 football season, attending graduate-level business courses to bolster his knowledge. During that 2010

QUICK FACT

When Wilson first came to NC State, he was the fourth or fifth quarterback on the Wolfpack's depth chart.

20 30 40 50 40 30 2

Wilson is shown here on his way to a 21-yard gain during a game against the Pittsburgh Panthers in 2009. He rushed for 260 yards over the course of that season.

season, Wilson led the ACC with 274.1 passing yards and 307.5 yards of total offense per game. He also became one of just four college football players to record more than 1,000 career rushing yards and more than 5,000 career passing yards. For his efforts, Wilson was voted the Governor's Award winner, or most valuable player, by his teammates.

QUICK FACT

In 2009 Wilson was named NC State's most valuable offensive back.

Switching Gears

What a lot of people might not know is that in 2010 Wilson was chosen by the Colorado Rockies in the fourth round of the Major League Baseball (MLB) draft. While Wilson was certainly an exceptional football player, he was also known as a gifted baseball player with a lot of raw talent as a second baseman. Wilson played in 32 games with the Tri-City Dust Devils—a Rockies' minor league team—and posted a .230 batting average along with two home runs and 11 runs batted in (RBI). While those certainly aren't eye-popping numbers, the fact that Wilson was even thought to be talented enough to be drafted by a major league team is impressive in itself. The baseball bug certainly bit Wilson. In January 2011, shortly after the end of his junior football season, he shocked a lot of people by deciding to attend spring training with the Rockies.

Wilson is shown here at the Colorado Rockies' spring training complex in Scottsdale, Arizona, in 2011.

Tom O'Brien, Wilson's football coach at NC State, expressed apprehension about Wilson's baseball commitment, but he also said that he respected his quarterback's decision. Just a few months later, it was announced that Wilson had been granted a release from his football scholarship, thus ending his career at NC State.

After going to spring training and working with the Colorado team, Wilson played 61 games with another Rockies' minor league team, the Asheville Tourists, during the spring and early summer of 2011. Wilson hit .228 with three homers and 15 RBIs during that span. Then he switched gears again. While months before it looked as though Wilson would end his football career and focus on baseball, it was announced on June 27, 2011, that he would be spending his last year of NCAA eligibility playing quarterback for the University of Wisconsin Badgers. And so the next chapter of Wilson's life began.

A Legend in the Making

Wilson couldn't have predicted it, but his decision to transfer to Wisconsin from NC State paved the way toward his later career. His outstanding senior season in the Big Ten raised his national profile and set him up for NFL success. Wilson's rapid rise at the pro level made him a Super Bowl champion and an NFL superstar by the age of just 25.

Leading the Badgers

Wilson immediately made an impact on the Badgers, throwing for 255 yards and two touchdowns to go with 62 rushing yards and a rushing touchdown in his first start—a 51–17 win against UNLV. One of his best performances at Wisconsin came in a 42–13 victory over Minnesota, when he completed 16 of 17 passes for 178 yards and four touchdowns. At the end of the regular season, Wilson was voted by

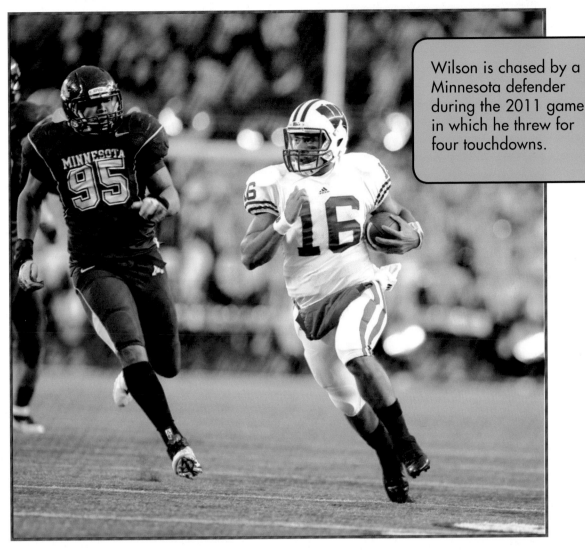

Wilson is chased by a Minnesota defender during the 2011 game in which he threw for four touchdowns.

both the coaches and the media as first-team All–Big Ten, and he was also awarded the Griese-Brees Big Ten Quarterback of the Year award. Wilson again put on a show in the Big Ten Championship game, when he threw for three touchdowns in a 42–39 win against the Michigan State Spartans. His efforts earned him yet another award, this time as the game's Grange-Griffin MVP.

Again being touted as one of college football's best players, Wilson was named third-team All-American by Yahoo! Sports and also finished ninth in the Heisman Trophy voting. (The Heisman Trophy is awarded

Wilson's last game as a Wisconsin Badger was an impressive one, as he threw for 296 yards and two touchdowns in a 45–38 loss to the Oregon Ducks at the 98th Rose Bowl.

each season to college football's best player.) In Wilson's final game as a Badger—the Rose Bowl—he again demonstrated some of his finest football skills. Throughout his high school and collegiate career, Wilson was known for stepping up and playing at a high level at big moments, and he certainly didn't disappoint in the Rose Bowl. Wilson completed 19 of 25 passes for 296 yards and two touchdowns, and he rushed for another score. Despite another great performance by the experienced quarterback, Wisconsin lost 45–38 in what would be Wilson's final game as both a Badger and a college football player. All in all, Wilson threw 33 touchdowns and ran for another six in his senior season while throwing only four interceptions and setting the NCAA Football Bowl Subdivision (FBS) record for passing efficiency, with an impressive 191.8 mark.

QUICK FACT

In an interview with ESPN, Wilson said that the biggest highlight from his college career was playing in the Rose Bowl.

NFL Beginnings

Following his successful season as a Wisconsin Badger, Wilson decided that he was going to commit full time to a career in the NFL, and he let the Colorado Rockies know that he wouldn't be reporting to 2012 spring training. Upon making that decision, Wilson began training for the NFL Scouting Combine. The combine is an event that measures a player's athletic ability and serves as a way for NFL scouts and coaches to get an idea of the type of talent a potential player possesses leading up to the NFL Draft, where teams select the players they want on their team. Before the 2012 draft, it was projected that Wilson would be a mid-round pick, with many analysts saying that he was too small to be a professional quarterback. According to the sports website SB Nation, the average height of quarterbacks taken in the first round between 2000 and 2009 was 6'4". Time and again, Wilson's height was an issue to those who underestimated his talent and heart.

Shortly after being drafted by the Seattle Seahawks in the third round of the NFL Draft on April 27, 2012—the 75th overall pick—Wilson began to prove that neither his height nor his draft location would determine his success in the NFL. Wilson signed a four-year, $2.99-million deal with the Seahawks and played well enough during the preseason to beat out both Matt Flynn and Tarvaris Jackson—both of whom had prior NFL experience—for the starting quarterback job in Seattle. Wilson's rookie season would be

QUICK FACT

In 2012 Wilson tied future Hall of Famer Peyton Manning for the most touchdown passes by an NFL rookie, with 26.

Wilson gets ready to pass during the 2012 NFL Scouting Combine. Wilson was drafted in the third round of the 2012 draft and went on to prove his critics wrong.

an extremely successful one. He led his team to the divisional round of the 2012 playoffs and was named Rookie of the Year for a season that was highlighted by more than 3,000 yards passing, 26 touchdown passes, 489 rushing yards, and four rushing touchdowns. Wilson was also voted to the Pro Bowl, which is the all-star game for the NFL.

Wilson dodges a Kansas City Chiefs safety during a 2012 game.

Winning Big

It was in Wilson's second pro season in 2013 that he cemented his status as a living legend not only in the NFL, but in the sports world in general. Wilson was once again voted to the Pro Bowl for a season in which he threw for 26 touchdowns to go with 3,357 passing yards, 539 rushing yards, and one rushing touchdown. Seattle went 13–3 during the regular season, tying the franchise record for best regular season record

It was the playoffs, though, that really mattered for Wilson's Seahawks, and they certainly didn't disappoint. After taking care of business against the New Orleans Saints in the divisional round and the San Francisco 49ers in the conference champion-ship, Seattle had a date with the Denver Broncos in Super Bowl XLVIII—arguably the

QUICK FACT

The Seahawks won their first-ever Super Bowl championship after the blowout against the Broncos.

Wilson holds up the Lombardi Trophy after the Seahawks' remarkable 43–8 win against Peyton Manning and the Denver Broncos in Super Bowl XLVIII.

biggest challenge of Wilson's young career. If it was a difficult challenge, it didn't faze Wilson or the Seahawks. On February 2, 2014, Seattle dismantled the Broncos, winning by the lopsided score of 43–8. Wilson completed 18 of 25 pass attempts and compiled 206 passing yards and two touchdowns on his way to helping Seattle win the Lombardi Trophy.

During the 2014 season, Wilson and the Seahawks again contended for the championship. After getting past the Carolina Panthers and Green Bay Packers in the playoffs, Seattle looked to win its second straight Super Bowl. But the team was unable to overcome Tom Brady and the New England Patriots, losing Super Bowl XLIX by a score of 28–24. Despite the loss— which resulted after Wilson threw an interception at the Patriots' goal line— Wilson continues to grow as a professional and learn from his mistakes to make himself the best player he can be.

Winning Off the Field

By now, you should have a good idea of who Russell Wilson is on the field. He's a gifted athlete and the starting quarterback of the Seattle Seahawks, but there's much more to the man than just his strong arm and quick legs. Wilson has grown into an exceptionally well-rounded man, both on the field and off. His father and grandfather were both well-educated athletes and respected men, and those qualities have been ingrained in Wilson as well. What most NFL fans don't know is that Wilson is also an incredibly charitable and kind-hearted individual.

QUICK FACT

In 2014—a year in which the NFL faced a multitude of domestic violence issues with its players—Wilson was one of the first players to speak out, saying, "This issue is much bigger than NFL suspensions. Domestic violence isn't going to disappear tomorrow or the next day. But the more that we choose not to talk about it, the more we shy away from the issue, the more we lose." In October 2014 he started the Why Not You Foundation to support victims of domestic violence.

20 | 30 | 40 | 50 | 40 | 30 | 20

Wilson (*right*) and his teammate Brandon Browner (*center*) donate their game-worn shoes to Samaritan's Feet, a charity supported by Carolina Panthers' wide receiver Steve Smith.

Paying It Forward

From the moment he was drafted by the Seahawks in 2012, it was apparent that Wilson was grateful for the opportunity to play professional football. One of the ways he expressed his gratitude was by helping others. He soon founded his own football camp, the Russell Wilson Passing Academy. In addition to teaching kids the fundamentals of football, the academy supports the mental and physical development of young people. The academy helps kids build character, learn sportsmanship, and establish moral standards all while learning the game. The creation of the Passing Academy is just

Wilson works with kids at his football camp, the Passing Academy.

QUICK FACT

Wilson hosts the Russell Wilson Passing Academy youth football camp in multiple cities during the off-season.

one of the many reasons why Wilson was awarded the Steve Largent Award in 2012, which is voted on by players and given to the Seahawk who best exemplifies dedication and integrity. The award is named after former Seattle wide receiver Steve Largent, who won the first award in 1989.

Wilson was just getting started when he developed his football camp. One thing that he loves to do is visit children in the hospital. On his off days during the NFL season—when most players are resting up for the upcoming game—Wilson spends his time at the Seattle Children's Hospital visiting with sick children and their families. Follow Wilson on Instagram or Facebook and your feed will be flooded with photographs of Wilson and smiling children in their hospital beds. This is what really makes Wilson a living legend. Of course we love his ability to make big plays on the football field, but his generosity and warm heart are what make him a great human being.

As part of his philanthropic efforts, Wilson is also heavily involved with the CR3 Diabetes Association, serving as its national ambassador. This nonprofit organization aids people who are suffering from diabetes by providing them with the supplies needed to keep them alive. Given the fact that Wilson lost his father to diabetes, it's easy to understand why he is so dedicated to helping people who suffer from the disease.

QUICK FACT

Wilson, in partnership with Verizon Wireless, has reached out to high school students to urge them to stop texting and driving.

During the 2013 season, Wilson leveraged his athletic ability to benefit his charitable nature when he teamed up with Russell Investments to earn money for his Power of Mind Foundation. The Power of Mind Foundation is a charity that raises funds for youth programs in underprivileged communities. Russell Investments pledged to make a donation to the foundation for every touchdown that Wilson scored that season. He wound up with 30 touchdowns, and Russell Investments

Wilson had a big year in 2013. With every touchdown, he both helped bring the Seahawks closer to the Super Bowl and raised money for underprivileged children.

donated $75,000 to his foundation. Wilson and Russell Investments continued their partnership in the 2014 season. The Power of Mind Foundation also held its first charity bowling event in 2013. In addition to Wilson himself, the event featured Felix Hernandez of MLB's Seattle Mariners and Wilson's Seahawk teammates Richard Sherman, Earl Thomas, Golden Tate, and Bobby Wagner.

Brand Ambassador

Even when he's not playing on Sundays, you'll still see Wilson multiple times per week on your television set. Wilson's athletic ability, combined with his likeable personality and generosity, has made him a favorite choice of brands looking for ambassadors for their products and services. Wilson has garnered multiple TV advertisement deals from some of the world's biggest brands, including Nike, Microsoft, Bose, Levi's, Duracell, Braun, United Way, and more. Not only does this show how popular Wilson has become to more than just football fans, it also reflects his character. Companies like Nike and Microsoft are extremely careful about whom they choose to represent them. As in the cases of athletes like Tiger Woods and Ray Rice, big brands have no issue cutting ties with their brand ambassadors if they've done something to negatively impact the

Wilson poses with some enthusiastic young fans at the Nickelodeon Kids' Choice Sports Awards in 2014.

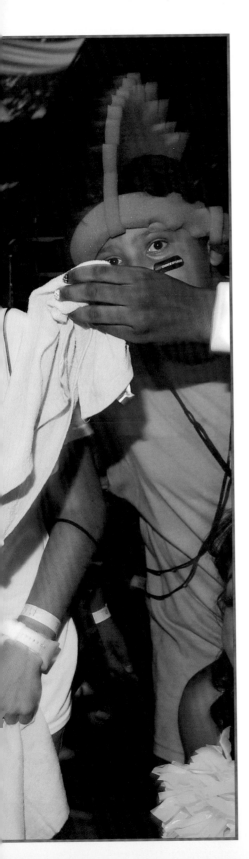

company's image. Wilson—who has never gotten into trouble off the field—is essentially the perfect cover boy for companies looking to promote their brand with a friendly face.

Although he excels at his job as quarterback of the Seattle Seahawks, Wilson's actions as a humanitarian are what ultimately make him a living legend. Through his charitable efforts and open-heartedness to the community, Wilson has become a role model and true champion, touching the lives of so many.

November 29, 1988: Russell Wilson is born in Cincinnati, Ohio.

July 23, 2006: Wilson commits to North Carolina State University, where he would spend three seasons at quarterback.

December 2, 2008: Wilson is named ACC Rookie of the Year after a stellar first season at NC State in which he threw for 1,955 yards passing, 17 touchdowns, and just one interception.

June 8, 2010: Wilson is drafted by the Colorado Rockies in the fourth round of the 2010 MLB draft.

June 9, 2010: Wilson's father, Harrison Wilson III, dies from diabetes.

June 27, 2011: Wilson transfers to the University of Wisconsin for his last year of NCAA eligibility.

January 2, 2012: Wilson leads the Wisconsin Badgers into the Rose Bowl, which they would lose 45–38 to the Oregon Ducks.

January 6, 2012: Wilson founds the Russell Wilson Passing Academy to help children ages 8–17 develop both football and life skills.

April 27, 2012: The Seattle Seahawks draft Russell Wilson as the 75th overall pick (12th pick of the third round) in the 2012 NFL Draft.

July 18, 2012: Wilson announces that he's partnered with the Power of Mind Foundation to help inner-city children.

February 2, 2013: Wilson is named NFL Rookie of the Year.

February 2, 2014: Wilson throws two touchdowns and leads the Seahawks to a 43–8 win over the Denver Broncos in Super Bowl XLVIII.

October 2014: Wilson speaks out about domestic violence in the NFL and launches the Why Not You Foundation.

February 1, 2015: Wilson and the Seahawks take on the New England Patriots in Super Bowl XLIX, losing 28–24.

Jim Brown (1936–) was the NFL's 1957 Rookie of the Year and led the league in rushing in eight of his nine seasons. He was voted to nine Pro Bowls, earned four MVP awards, and was inducted into the Pro Football Hall of Fame in 1971.

Joe Montana (1956–), longtime San Francisco 49ers' quarterback, led the team to four Super Bowl championships. Montana was also voted to the Pro Bowl eight times, was named Super Bowl MVP three times, was named NFL MVP in 1989 and 1990, and was inducted into the Hall of Fame in 2000.

John Elway (1960–) quarterbacked for the Denver Broncos from 1983 to 1998. He is a two-time Super Bowl champion, a nine-time Pro Bowler, the 1987 MVP, and a 2004 Hall of Fame inductee.

Michael Strahan (1971–) played defensive end for the New York Giants and holds the NFL record for most sacks in a single season (22.5). He is a seven-time Pro Bowler and a Defensive Player of the Year winner (2001), and he won a Super Bowl with the Giants in his last season in 2007. He was inducted into the Hall of Fame in 2014.

Peyton Manning (1976–) holds the NFL record for most touchdown passes in a single season (55). He is also a Super Bowl champion and MVP, five-time NFL MVP, and 13-time Pro Bowler.

Tom Brady (1977–), the quarterback of the New England Patriots, is a four-time Super Bowl champion and a two-time Super Bowl MVP, nine-time Pro Bowler, and two-time NFL MVP.

Drew Brees (1979–), the New Orleans Saints' quarterback, is an eight-time Pro Bowler, a Super Bowl champion and MVP, and two-time NFL Offensive Player of the Year.

Eli Manning (1981–) is the brother of Peyton and quarterback of the New York Giants. He has led the Giants to two Super Bowl championships, winning the MVP award in both of them, and has been voted to three Pro Bowls.

GLOSSARY

ambassador An official representative or messenger.

charity An organization that helps people in need.

devout Devoted to religion or to religious duties or exercises.

diabetes A serious disease in which the body cannot properly control the amount of sugar in the blood because it does not have enough insulin.

domestic violence The inflicting of physical injury by one family or household member on another.

Football Bowl Subdivision The top division of football at the college level.

franchise Of or relating to a team that is a member of a professional sports league.

humanitarian A person who works to make other people's lives better.

integrity Total honesty and sincerity.

Lombardi Trophy Named after former NFL player and coach Vince Lombardi, the Lombardi Trophy is the prize that an NFL team receives for winning the Super Bowl.

MLB Major League Baseball. It is the major North American professional baseball organization that was formed in 1903 with the merger of the two U.S. professional baseball leagues—the National League (NL) and the American League (AL).

NCAA National Collegiate Athletic Association, which is the association that organizes and controls athletic programs for colleges and universities across the United States.

NFL National Football League. It is the major U.S. professional gridiron football organization, founded in 1920 in Canton, Ohio, as the American Professional Football Association.

NFL Draft An annual event in which NFL teams select college football players to play for them.

NFL Scouting Combine A weeklong event where college football players show their mental and physical skills to NFL teams who may be looking to draft them.

philanthropic Charitable; humanitarian.

Pro Bowl The NFL's version of an all-star game in which the players are voted on by coaches, fans, and their peers.

redshirt To keep a college athlete out of competition for a year in order to extend eligibility.

rookie A first-year player in a professional sport.

Super Bowl The annual championship game in the NFL between the top teams from the AFC and the NFC.

FOR MORE INFORMATION

Books

Anderson, Jameson. *Russell Wilson*. Minneapolis, MN: ABDO, 2015.

Fishman, Jon M. *Russell Wilson*. Minneapolis, MN: Lerner Publishing, 2015.

Gilbert, Sara. *The Story of the NFL*. Mankato, MN: Creative Education, 2012.

Kelley, K.C. *Football Superstars 2014*. New York, NY: Scholastic, 2014.

Scheff, Matt. *Best NFL Quarterbacks of All Time*. Minneapolis, MN: ABDO, 2014.

Thiel, Art, and Steve Rudman. *Russell Wilson: Standing Tall*. Chicago, IL: Triumph Books, 2014.

Websites

Because of the changing nature of Internet links, Rosen Publishing has developed an online list of websites related to the subject of this book. This site is updated regularly. Please use this link to access this list:

http://www.rosenlinks.com/LLS/Wil

INDEX